With God All Things Are Possible!

Copyright © 2016

All rights reserved

ISBN 978-0-9983078-3-1
ISBN 0998307831

All rights reserved. No part of this publication may be reproduced in any means, in any way, without the permission, in writing, from the Copyright owner. A product of Skookum Books
864 552 1055

Dedication: This writing is for our oldest, first-born son, Jim! For his love, all he wanted in return, was love and approval! He gave freely, to everyone, and asked for nothing in return. He gave us wonderful memories of his musical talent. His quartet played many times, at many places, and brought fun and joy to many people! He played the piano beautifully, and was fun to be with. Everyone wanted to be on his team in Trivial Pursuit! He would be elated with these writings being produced!

Acknowledgement: To my many students, a great big thank you for the good things you gave to me! I loved those years of teaching in Sandusky, Ohio. I enjoyed working for The Sandusky School System and was proud being associated with all the fine people there!

 Skookum Book's Charms!

The beautiful butterfly, that graces our flowers and bushes, goes through a mysterious and magical change in becoming an adult! The Greeks believed each time a butterfly emerges from it's cocoon, a new human soul is born! Legend has it that whispering a wish to a butterfly, then releasing it to carry the wish to heaven, will make the wish come true! Perhaps this is when they acquire little clouds on their wings! The butterfly is a symbol of fresh lIfe, happiness, and joy! The "night butterfly", the moth, is attracted to a flame and light, just like our souls are attracted to heavenly truths!

Hummingbirds are active, beautiful additions to our gardens, who give us a sense of life! These "flying jewels" flit from flower to flower, picking up and delivering pollen, so that life can continue. Hummingbirds open the heart and show the truth of beauty. It brings laughter and enjoyment and the magic of being alive! The hummingbird stands for spreading love and joy!

Proverbs: The First Book Written For The Young,
And a Little Bit for Everyone!

Betty Lou Rogers

Illustrated by:
Jenison Hardin

Have you ever wondered which book,
Was first written to help the youth?
Proverbs was written to guide and inform,
To show common sense, good manners, and truth!

Proverbs tell what wise people will do,
They'll look for whatever is good,
Importance, to them, isn't money or fame,
But caring for others, where kindness remains!

Solomon was a king, who lived long ago,
He's been called the wisest on earth,
His friendly advice is to teach and to guide,
And lead young people to value their worth!

Solomon was like a father to the young,
He wanted to help them excel,
He wanted to show the pitfalls ahead,
And learn from the lessons of life as well!

Solomon became a wise old man,
King David was his dad,
God granted him his heart's desire,
To be a wise man, and shun the bad!

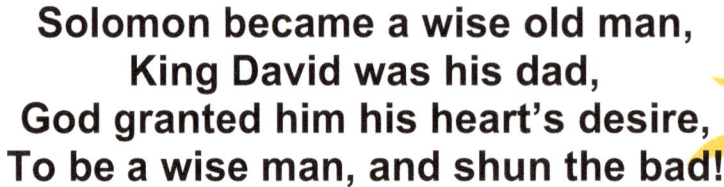

The Book of Proverbs speaks of everyday life,
It gives good advice - -, how to live,
It comes from wise experience,
It focuses on God, and all his gifts!

Do you want a prosperous life, young man?
Fasten loyalty around your neck,
Write faithfulness upon your heart,
Refuse wrong acts, and show respect!

Have you ever met a "know it all"?
They'll take no advice, none-at-all,
They think they know more than they do,
And they end up being the great big fool!

Praise tests a person as heat tests metal,
How do you stand up under heat?
Do you need approval for a job well done?
Or do you quietly help till all is won?

Going after something you have to have,
Is a trap that has jaws like steel,
Makes you think you cannot live without,
These desires are awful, but real!

The pathway to wisdom is common sense,
It's paved with right choices and trust,
We must keep ourselves free of pride and greed,
As God gives us freedom to do what we must!

Leaning, resting, and trusting in God,
Is the way wise decisions are made,
God knows what is the best for us,
We must look for His guidance and aid!

Insecure, uncertain people have something to prove,
They doubt themselves, while hiding it from all,
They also have a need to show themselves off,
And when they do, the show is quite small!

Prudent people have nothing to prove,
They're secure in all that they are,
What they say and do is straight from the heart,
Their desires and needs are unselfish by far!

Are you a pain-relieving person?
Or are you the source of pain and grief?
Being cheerful, greeting others with a smile,
Is a tonic, sure to last, a good long while!

Proud people don't know where they're weak,
Nor where their problems lie,
They don't see themselves as "common",
And don't know their problem is pride!

There are many benefits to keeping your mouth shut,
Especially if you have nothing worthy to say,
It gives you a chance to listen and learn,
And if you're a fool, you won't give it away!

There are people who need only you,
Everyone needs someone who cares,
In good times and bad, nothing else will suffice,
But a friend with whom you can share!

Dishonesty, God really despises,
He hates when he has to disown,
We all should want truth, never sell it,
While we remain true to God alone!

An honest person has value and honor,
And gives comfort, assurance, and trust,
Dishonest gains can't bring contentment and rest,
Better to live with much less, if you must!

Plotting to commit evil is so horrid,
Where do these evil desires begin?
In a heart and soul that is empty of love,
And a brain that's unused, filled with sin!

Evil desires are so senseless,
When put into action, there's pain,
What fool has the right to stop heart beats?
And ruin people's lives through deceit!

The righteous are hopeful and helpful,
Wicked people's actions are cruel,
The righteous stand firm, and delight in what's good,
The wicked have trouble, because they're the fool!

The more you love and respect our God,
The less you'll accept evil ways,
Hating pride, lies, and foolishness,
The safer our world will remain!

Everyday has twenty-four hours,
Hours to treasure for the chances it gives,
You can choose to help out and serve others,
Work hard, don't waste time, as you live!

People can be a construction opportunity,
Or they can be a nasty demolition site,
Everyone has weapons that easily destroy,
They also have tools to build and delight!

Give freely of all your energy,
Your time, and all that you hold,
For when you give, you also get,
Great riches, far greater than gold!

A half an ounce of good advice,
Has more worth, than a ton of bad,
It's easy to spout off thoughtless remarks,
That lead to confusion, and make people sad!

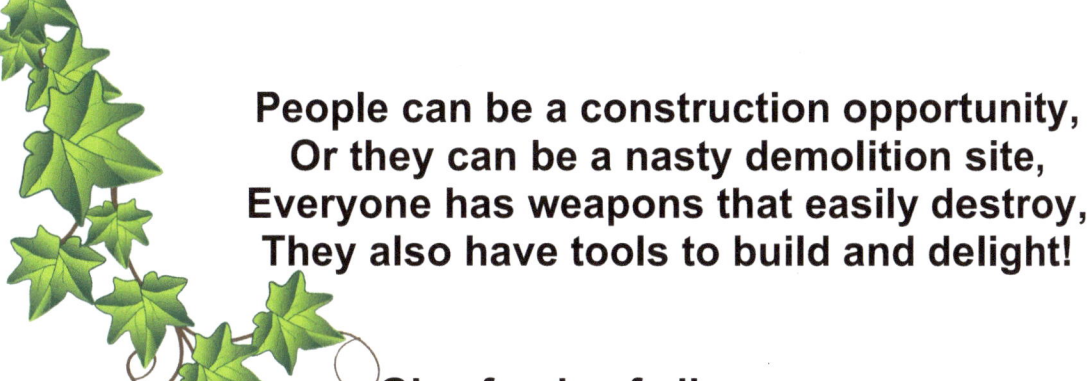

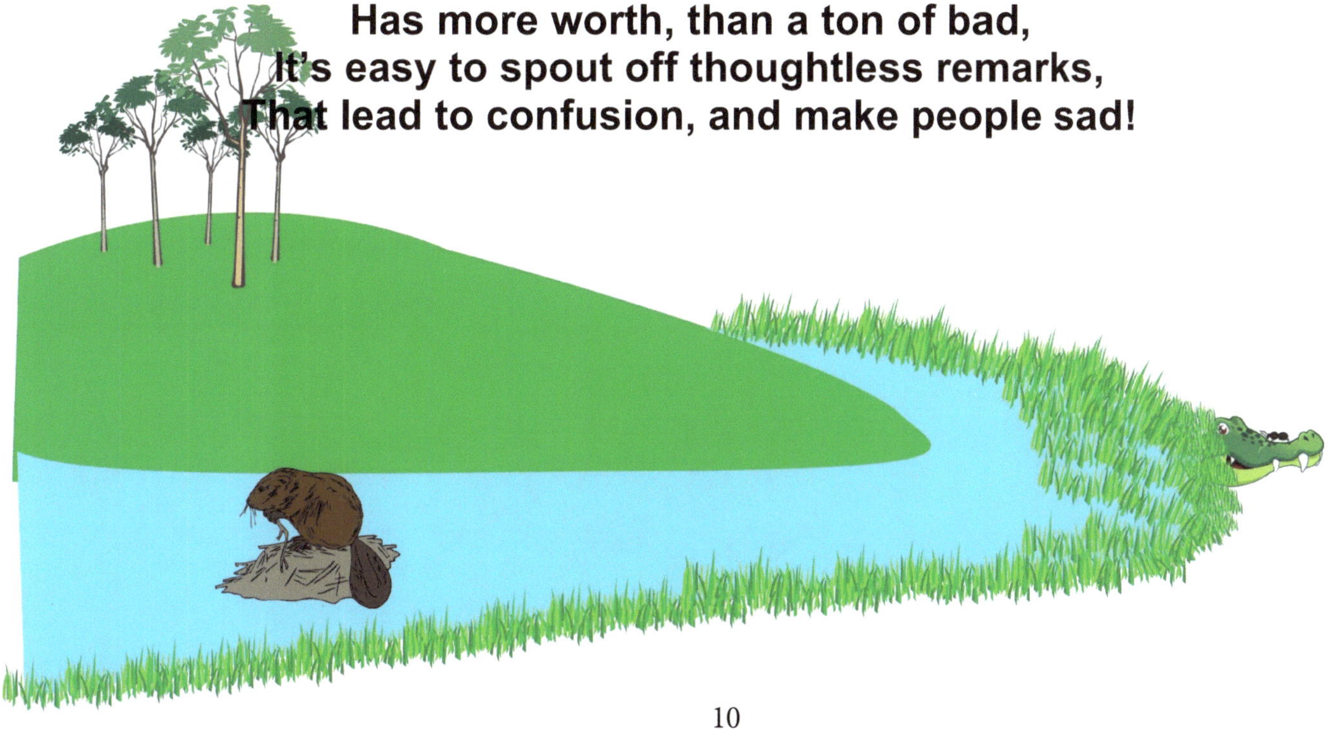

Knowledge is good, it's having the facts,
And wisdom guides what we should do,
To have the facts without wisdom to guide,
Is dangerous and dumb, through and through!

If you have no wish to learn,
You will remain a fool,
Accept advice from learned men,
And know it's wise to follow rules!

Evil choices cause your life to destruct,
Right choices lead toward good,
It doesn't make sense to want what is bad,
Choose safety over ruin, choose would over could!

Spend time with people you want to be like,
Because you'll grow up being just like them,
A rotten apple spoils the rest of the fruit,
Get rid of what's spoiled, and keep the gems!

It isn't easy to be a mother and dad,
For at times they have to be stern,
Parents bring children into this world,
Now they must teach, what children should learn!

The wise person helps and gives good advice,
The fool doesn't change, stays uncouth,
The wise person wants to learn even more,
The fool blames and lies about truth!

Anger is good used against every wrong,
A quick temper's a fire out of control,
Anger's a selfish response when accused,
Makes dishonesty appear as a goal!

Feeding our minds and our bodies,
Should cause some people concern,
The films we watch, the music we hear,
Makes us what we are, and for what we yearn!

Whatever you do in this life as you live,
Commit to the Lord, all you do,
Trust God as if everything depended on Him,
While working, like all things depended on you!

Would you have your wishes come true,
Or would you rather your fears?
Wishes come from desires of the heart,
Fears come from lack of faith, my dears!

Now, as you meet with elder ones,
You should treat them with respect,
For they have lived more years than you,
So what you see, is what you'll get!

The gray hair and the wrinkled skin,
Are signs of work and wear,
Our elders show some lessons learned,
They've weathered experiences beyond compare!

Whatever kind of friend are you?
Through foul weather well as fair?
A true friend shows real loyalty,
With support and unselfish care!

As our Creator, God values us all,
Whether we're rich or poor, bad or good,
When we help someone out, we honor God!
Both our Creator, and His Creation, as we should!

Parents, train your children well,
So when they leave your tidy nest,
They'll make the choices you have shown,
They'll do the things that are the best!

People who are eager to learn,
Listen well and become wiser as they grow,
As they experience the challenges in life,
They're better prepared as the problems arise!

Do not envy wicked men,
Their hearts are full of hate,
They have nothing at all that's worth your time,
For their lips impart only dirt and grime!

The caring tongue speaks out for truth,
The careless tongue spits out such lies,
The conniving tongue has a deceitful heart,
The controlled tongue gives sound advice!

An out-of-control life, is open to sin,
It's agreeing that "anything goes",
By choosing, planning, and picking what's good,
Keeps you safe, ready, and in control!

We should not seek rewards for ourselves,
Instead, serve all with gladness of heart,
Loud-mouths and liars have one thing in mind,
To put on a show - - -, and there's no good part!

The man who drinks, and drinks too much,
Is miserable and a sorry sight,
His bruises show outside and in,
And he hurts as if a snake did bite!

Those who want to kill and destroy,
Will be caught in a trap of their own,
For ashes and dust are the rubble they leave,
In which nothing good can be grown!

Happy are those under righteous rule,
An honest ruler has a nation so strong,
Wicked rule causes misery and strife,
When fame is first, there's no meaning to life!

A greedy desire comes from Satan,
When you want, and can't live without,
It will eat and finally consume you,
And leave you unfit, full of doubt!

Everyone makes mistakes in life,
But only fools will repeat them,
The only time mistakes are good,
Is, if you learn, and beat them!

Parents grow weary of parenting,
They want to be good to their kids,
When they nag, scold, and limit kids actions,
It's because parents want their kids satisfaction!

For a government or society to last,
Leaders need to be wise and informed,
But if leaders make foolish decisions,
The nation will weaken and be scorned!

A person who shows real wisdom,
Is loving and patient and kind,
Gives good advice, has common sense,
Believes in God, keeps others in mind!

Facts are facts. and that's a fact,
They shouldn't be twisted, changed, or spun,
And if they are, like some fools will do,
They're turned into lies, and no longer true!

Troublesome times can be useful,
They will show just who you are,
For any trouble you work out today,
Tomorrow, you'll be wiser, by far!

"I deserve this" is a deadly sin,
It appeals to the empty heart,
If you fill that hollow place with love,
You'll find better ideas to impart!

"I need this", is another deadly sin,
It appeals to the empty head,
Wisdom can fill that vacant place,
'Twill help you find what others need, instead!

Trust, once sacrificed, is hard to regain,
True trust seldom gets a second chance,
So, protect this hallowed human trait,
Be honorable and worthy, at any rate!

The height of arrogance in our world today,
Are those who think they're in charge,
In charge of life, who lives? who dies?
Those heads are filled with vicious lies!

It's so wrong for a judge to be biased,
It's unfair saying the guilty are not,
When the innocent are charged as if guilty,
Perhaps a small bribe sealed the plot!

Truth, wisdom, learning, and good sense,
Are qualities worth accepting in life,
Because of their value, you never should sell,
Living God's way, takes hard work just as well!

The dangers and hazards of harmful acts,
Are so wrong, they degrade the soul,
They erode all sense of human-ness,
While leading one into a demon's hole!

A man who is guilty of murder,
Is digging his grave, hand by hand,
So, don't even try to stop him,
'Cause he's digging as fast as he can!

Wickedness can be intoxicating and hypnotic,
One wicked deed can lead to another,
Until all thought of what's truly good,
Is completely forgotten and misunderstood!

Satan is at work when he plants the wish
For the greedy desire for self,
If you let this grow, it will bloom and destroy,
Better to help others, and watch them enjoy!

Gossip is so tasty,
We love to share and tell,
While a lie is sour and nasty,
Making truth like caramel!

When people crave satisfaction,
These desires cause unhappiness,
Especially if what you're craving,
Is not what's good and blest!

If you seek guidance to goodness,
The ideas will flow like a stream,
Feelings like you're in heaven,
Will cover you as in a dream!

Truthfulness lasts forever,
God's character also endures,
The Bible is The Book of Life,
Because God is Truth, and God is sure!

Don't wait to discipline a child,
They have to learn to behave,
Saying "no" is not going to kill them,
Might even begin a new trend!

Freedom doesn't mean "free for all",
To our founders it meant free to live,
Free to live under God, and His God-given rights,
And not just to take, but to give all you might!

Free-will allows humans the power to choose,
How to behave, how to think, how to select,
But being a slave to the sins of our world,
Chains you up, not the life you'd expect!

The mouth of a fool invites ruin,
The wicked are punished by their pay,
Now the lips of the righteous feed many,
They rejoice in perfection and grace

When someone is charged with breaking a rule,
Their response is, "You just don't like me,"
"I like you, but what you did was wrong!"
If it continues, you'll hear the same old song!

Wisdom appeals at first to the mind,
Folly appeals to one's feelings,
Since feelings are easy to excite,
The mind should control all the dealings!

Mouths of fools spew out much hate,
While tongues of the wise will commend,
The head of a fool, it does not think,
A wise head will think, then condemn!

A loving person, lives their love,
A faithful person, shows their faith,
A truthful person, will not lie,
A Godly person, believes in grace!

The one great thing we all must do,
Above all else, guard your heart,
Keep those desires that spread the love,
And know that it comes from up above!

Look at the ant as it toils and stores,
It needs rest at the end of the day,
Like the ant, we too must be willing to work,
To provide for, and earn our own way!

God gives wisdom to those who seek,
What's right, and just, and fair,
He wants what's good for everyone,
He wants righteousness everywhere!

Parents be aware, you're being watched,
Your children are learning about life,
They have to choose between goodness and sin,
They have to know what's true, real, and genuine!

The person who has no purpose in life,
Is wandering and supposedly lost,
Beware of temptations that lead one astray.
Like lambs to the slaughter, you're going the wrong way!

Excuses, lies, and alibis,
Are cowardly actions to claim,
These people would rather accuse someone else,
Than admit a mistake, and take the blame!

The wicked messenger falls into trouble,
When he doesn't stay true to the truth,
A faithful envoy speaks out words of healing,
When he gives the story the right kind of feeling!

An evil-doer listens to wicked lips,
A liar, to a destructive tongue,
Laughing at a calamity is so unfeeling,
These ugly pitfalls leave young ones reeling!

The ideal woman in our world,
Is strong, smart, and trusts in God,
She works so hard, she's kind and free,
She's an inspiration, she's the best she can be!

Now when you grow weary, and full of doubt,
You want to be someone worth noting,
So, what do you do, when you feel so defeated?
"Treat others the way you'd like to be treated"!

And always remember, never forget - - -

America is your homeland,
'Twas won with blood and strife,
And cherish all our freedoms,
And guard them with your life!

About the Author

Betty Lou Rogers is a retired fourth grade teacher from Madison Elementary School in Sandusky, Ohio. Her strategy for success was simple. Engage! Work together! Be active learners! Then employ her "one more chance" philosophy! Betty Lou Rogers grew up in rural northwestern Ohio, graduating from Fremont Ross High School. She married her childhood sweetheart and raised three sons. During this time, she returned to college where she graduated with a B. S. Degree in Elementary Education from Bowling Green State University, in Bowling Green, Ohio. She was a member of the prestigious educational society, Kappa Delta Pi. While teaching at Madison School, Mrs. Rogers was keenly aware of what children needed, both as a group and as individuals, in effectual learning in the classroom. She also had the intuition to know how to accomplish this by challenging her students to be active learners, as opposed to the sit, listen, and absorb approach! Always have lesson material in front of the student, so they are actively participating in the lesson, never pushing the child beyond their ability, but always working toward the best they can do! Often times the student is awakened to and surprised by their own ability. Mrs. Rogers' most telling educational approach was offering the children "one more chance" to learn and succeed, by giving open-book tests!

Tests show what the student hasn't learned! "My job is to give the children every opportunity to learn." This strategy caused her students to become more familiar with the contents and location of information in their books. This offering, enabled them to find the answer, complete the test, and learn what was missed before. These answers could even be more meaningful to them! When parents found this out, there was no excuse for a failing grade!

Mrs. Rogers was also a Jennings Scholar, which honored and rewarded teachers in the elementary classroom. The Jennings Foundation provides a means for greater accomplishment, on the part of teachers, with the hope it would result in greater recognition for those in the teaching profession within the public school system.

Mrs. Rogers is a member of Advent United Methodist Church in Simpsonville, S.C. Besides writing, she loves her sewing and crafts, and gardening! Mrs. Rogers and her husband have four granddaughters, and seven great-grandchildren!

After twenty-seven years of teaching, Mrs. Rogers philosophy for success has permeated the American landscape through her students in both academic and professional fields. Her love for teaching and writing, can never be equaled in any way, except her hope for students to find her writing truly illuminating!

Mrs. Rogers' previously published works:

The Thimseagle Thievers

Change Can Be Good!

Paste and Gluey, A Sticky Tale!

New publications coming:

Kate Earns Her MBA in Manners, Behavior, Attitude!

Chris Earns His MBA in Manners, Behavior, Attitude!

A new series of books for preteens and teens:

It's So Important To Be Honest!

The Ten Commandments for Teens, and Helpful Hints In-Between!

Proverbs, The First Book Written For the Young, Plus A Little Bit For Everyone! Acquiring The Human Skills of Thinking, Saying, and Doing, for Teens!

A Medley of Options for the "Not Yet Old" Set!

God and Country. Two Sets of Laws For Teens!

The Human Dilemma of the Young, The Scramble for PAM! Power, Approval, and Money, (Ecclesiastes)

A Hodge-Podge of Thoughts For Teens, That's Not Gibberish!

Law and Order for Teens: Ignore or Restore!

ABC's For Teens, and What They Mean!

So, You Think We Shouldn't Have Dropped "The Bomb"?

For fun: Bossy Susie Saucy   and   Capricious Caleb O'Connor

Proverbs: The First Book Written for the Young, With a Little Bit for Everyone! Is about the thoughts, feelings, advice, and quips King Soloman gave for the benefit of young people! Some are funny, but all true.

Other published works by Betty Lou Rogers:

Chis Earns His MBA in Manners, Behavior, Attitude!
Kate Earns Her MBA in Manners, Behavior, Attitude!
The Ten Commandments for Teens, and Helpful Hints In-Betwwen

It's So Important To Be Honest!
The Thimseagle Thievers
Change Can Be Good!
Paste and Gluey, A Sticky Tale!

Mrs. Rogers books are published under:
Skookum Books.com

www.ingramcontent.com/pod-product-compliance
Lightning Source LLC
Chambersburg PA
CBHW041225040426
42444CB00002B/55